LIVING THE LABYRINTH

D0102976

living the

LABYRINTH

101 paths to a deeper connection with the sacred

Jill Kimberly Hartwell Geoffrion

THE PILGRIM PRESS

CLEVELAND, OHIO

This work is dedicated to all those who have yet to experience a labyrinth.

The Pilgrim Press, Cleveland, Ohio 44115
© 2000 by Jill Kimberly Hartwell Geoffrion

Grateful acknowledgment for the following: From Laurie Goodstein, "Reviving Labyrinths, Paths to Inner Peace," *New York Times*, May 10, 1998. Copyright © 1998 by the New York Times Co. Reprinted by permission. ⋅ From Battle A. Beasley, "A Labyrinth Journey," *The Source* 5 (fall 1997): 7. Reprinted by permission.

The eleven-circuit Chartres labyrinth pattern is assumed throughout this book. While designed with a Chartres-style labyrinth in mind, most of the exercises can be used with a seven-circuit, "classical" labyrinth. The labyrinth pattern used here is the most accurate representation available of the Chartres labyrinth as drawn by Robert Ferré and used with his permission.

Biblical quotations, unless otherwise noted, are from the New Revised Standard Version of the Bible, © 1989 by the Division of Christian Education of the National Council of Churches of Christ in the U.S.A., and are used by permission. Adaptations may have been made for inclusivity.

Library of Congress Cataloging-in-Publication Data

Geoffrion, Jill Kimberly Hartwell, 1958–
      Living the labyrinth : 101 paths to a deeper connection with the sacred / Jill Kimberly Hartwell Geoffrion.
          p. cm.
      Includes bibliographical references.
      ISBN 0-8298-1372-1 (pbk. : alk. paper)
      1. Spiritual life—Christianity.   2. Labyrinths—Religious aspects—Christianity.   3. Meditations.   4. Labyrinths—Religious aspects—Christianity—Meditations.   I. Title.
BV4509.5.G447 2000
248.4'6—dc21
                                                                99-054633

C o n t e n t s

Foreword ix
Acknowledgments xiii
Diagram of Chartres-Style Labyrinth xiv
Introduction xv

Part 1   Journeys to Creativity

1   Creative Travel 2
2   Lighting the Way 2
3   When You Have Time 3
4   Stoking the Fire 4
5   Going for a Walk 4

Part 2   The Sum Is More Than the Parts

6   Walking into Answers 6
7   Near or Far? 6
8   Closing a Circle 7
9   Inside Out 7
10   Turning 8
11   Circling In and Out 8
12   Circumambulating 9
13   Crossing 10
14   Holy Meanderings 11
15   Walking outside the Lines 11
16   Back to the Center 12
17   Threshold Moments 12
18   Walking the Lunations 13

Part 3   Being with Others at the Labyrinth

19   Looking in the Mirror 16
20   Processional Walking 16
21   Sharing the Space 17

Contents

22 Interceding for Others 18
23 Seeing Deeply 19
24 A New Context for an Established Group 19
25 Following and Leading 20
26 Perfect Photo Opportunities 21
27 Introducing One Friend to Another 22
28 Differing Perceptions 23
29 Reconnecting 23

Part 4   This Could Happen to You

30 Going Back . . . to Go Forward 26
31 Interrupting the Flow 26
32 One Step at a Time 27
33 Before or after a Funeral 28

Part 5   Embodied Explorations

34 Clap Your Hands 30
35 Restricting and Freeing Yourself 30
36 Internal Labyrinths 31
37 Close Your Eyes 32
38 Following Sacred Nudgings 32
39 Paying Attention to Your Body 33
40 Be a Snail 34
41 Why Not Play on the Labyrinth?! 34
42 What Would Happen 35
43 Knowing Feet 35
44 Backing Away/Towards 36
45 Moving 37
46 Do You Want to Dance? 38
47 Pacing Yourself 38
48 Following Ancient Pilgrims 38
49 Memorial Day 39
50 Zeroing In 40

Part 6   Intentional Encounters with the Divine

51 Being Drawn In 42
52 Moving with Your Center 42
53 Nesting 43

54	Thanks Giving	43
55	Your Offering	43
56	Communicating with Your Body	44
57	Letting Go	44
58	Surprise Rendezvous	45
59	Sacred Offerings	46
60	Worshiping	46

Part 7   Experiencing Outdoor Labyrinths

61	Moon Gazing	48
62	Whispered Truths	48
63	Awesome Wondering	49
64	Reaching In and Out	49

Part 8   Opening to Wisdom

65	Praying a Question	52
66	Remembering	53
67	Journaling All the Way	53
68	Reworking and Rejoicing	54
69	Role Playing	55
70	Spiritual Traveling Companions	56
71	Walking a Question through the Four Seasons	57
72	Happy Birthday	57
73	Shedding	58

Part 9   Biblical Meditations for Labyrinth Praying

74	Exploring the Valley of the Shadow of Death · Psalm 23:4	60
75	Praying the Lord's Prayer · Matthew 6:9–13	61
76	Grounded, Rooted, and Growing · Jeremiah 17:7–8	61
77	Praying for Someone in Need · Ephesians 6:18	62
78	Resting · Matthew 11:28	63
79	Thanksgiving · Psalm 9:1–2	64
80	The Wide Open Path · 2 Samuel 22:33	65
81	A Mind to Understand, Eyes to See, Ears to Hear · Deuteronomy 29:2–4	65
82	Refreshment · Revelation 21:5–6	66
83	Your Will Be Done · Matthew 6:10	67

84   The Fruit of Walking the Labyrinth 68
        · Galatians 5:22–23

85   An Oasis in the Desert · Psalm 107:35 69

86   Sacred Formation · Isaiah 44:2 69

87   Like a Little Child · Mark 10:13–16 70

Part 10   Let Your Fingers Do the Walking

88   Walking the Labyrinth by Hand 72

89   Being Rocked 73

90   Fingering 74

91   Coloring 74

Part 11   Try This!

92   When Upset 76

93   Walking and Resting 76

94   Gaining Knowledge, Gaining Wisdom 77

95   Working with a Dream 77

96   Tuning In 78

97   Being Here 79

98   Spiritual Exploring 79

99   Sweep Your Way to the Center 80

100   Coming Together 80

101   Caring 81

      Labyrinth Resources 83

      Bibliography 85

Foreword

The labyrinth is an effective spiritual tool, generic in nature, and personal in application. Most people who walk a labyrinth see the metaphor at once: it is like the twists and turns of their journey through life. This analogy can be carried further: The way we walk the labyrinth both reflects and affects how we see ourselves and our world.

Author Jill Geoffrion is a mystic. She walks with God. Her approach to the labyrinth brings to mind a concept of Pierre Teilhard de Chardin called the Omega Point. He proposes that the divine is available and accessible to us, not by our seeking it outside of ourselves, but by our going within. We go deeper and deeper within until we come to the point at which we encounter Truth, at which we encounter All That Is.

As Geoffrion knows full well, the labyrinth can lead us to ourselves, and thus to God. It is for this reason that *Living the Labyrinth* is so valuable. It is a guidebook not just for walking labyrinths, but for turning our lives into a sacred pilgrimage.

Labyrinths are unicursal, having a single path. With no choices or intersections, that path leads unfailingly (though circuitously) to the center. Mazes, on the other hand, have multiple paths and myriad choices, most of which lead nowhere. As a literary motif and allegory, the labyrinth is almost universally confused with a maze as a symbol for difficult entry or exit, for disorientation and complexity, or as a metaphor of the human condition. This confusion between labyrinths and mazes is evident in most dictionaries, which define each one as the other.

There is, in fact, a big difference experientially. Life-as-maze and life-as-labyrinth are opposite concepts, mutually exclusive, with vastly different metaphysical premises. In a maze we lose ourselves, in a labyrinth we find ourselves. A maze often involves a physical and mental contest between the walker and the maze designer, in the end producing not just losers but victims, failure at the hands of someone else. In a labyrinth there is no competition; we can relax the intellect and be present with the journey itself, establishing our connection to the sacred.

Although most of us acknowledge the desirability of labyrinths, when it comes down to it, we generally see our lives as mazes, not labyrinths. It is easy to feel that we are off the path, that success is not assured, or that it comes only with luck and struggle. We see many of the decisions or events in our lives not as turns but as dead ends, time wasted, money lost, opportunities missed. We reprimand ourselves when we are divorced, or downsized, or if we fail as parents. Our rational minds work overtime. These are all traits of a maze, not a labyrinth.

Our tendency to view life as a maze is largely societal. Many institutional religions describe earthly life as a maze, with only a few chosen people making it through to eternal reward. Much formal schooling consists of little more than learning to choose the right answers, thereby dividing the world into right (paths) and wrong (paths), success and failure. Advertisers bombard us with the message that we are on the wrong path, with dire consequences unless we buy the right product.

Our spiritual quest, I feel, can be summarized as this single obligation: to switch from life-as-maze to life-as-labyrinth. The transformation from maze to labyrinth requires us to dismiss much of our conditioning, to reevaluate our identity, and to apply a new context to our lives. With life-as-labyrinth, we discover that all paths are part of the One Path, leading unfailingly to the center, where, despite appearances and differences, we will eventually all meet. No one will be lost. If we are alive, we *are* on the path.

The logic of living the labyrinth frees us from the onerous nature of choices. We can go in one direction or its opposite. We are opened to a wide range of possibilities without the fear that our choices will cause us to be lost or constitute a dead end. We can marry or not marry, drive a new car or an old one, do work that we find satisfying, determine the direction of our spiritual path, pick among possible investments and future scenarios. Living the labyrinth means operating from a position of free choice rather than obligation.

Connecting with the sacred involves trusting the process, continuing to move forward on the path step by step. Skill comes into play not to make our choices, but to enhance the quality of our following the path. Therein lies the value of this book. I know no one who treads the labyrinth's luminous paths with more surrender and confidence and conviction than author Jill Kimberly Hartwell Geoffrion. She knows the difference between life-as-maze and life-as-labyrinth.

With courage and devotion, Geoffrion truly lives the labyrinth. Consider her advice: "Give thanks for where your walk has brought you. ... Notice the feelings, thoughts, memories, and sensations that accompany you. ... Find an embodied way to express your gratefulness. ... Welcome the wisdom and images which come. ... Pray the prayers that are in your heart."

Geoffrion's four-step formula is straightforward: Ask, listen, receive, be grateful. This is important advice, for the labyrinth and for life. Writing in a poetic prose, she offers her suggestions gently, respectfully, joyfully. Nowhere will we find a more creative guide than *Living the Labyrinth*.

Robert Ferré

Acknowledgments

What a wondrous journey labyrinth praying is! My explorations with the labyrinth have been supported and enhanced by:

God,
ever present, full of surprises, inviting growth at every turn;

Tim Geoffrion,
my husband, whose insights on my manuscript have consistently stretched and supported me;

Kate Christianson,
whose faithful prayers have provided a steady foundation for my work;

Elizabeth Nagel,
with whom I have been developing and co-teaching material on the labyrinth and the enneagram;

Robert Ferré,
whose leadership on my pilgrimages to Chartres prepared the ground for deep transformation;

Lauren Artress,
from whom I have learned much about labyrinth facilitation;

Liz Lapour,
whose practical help allowed me to keep my focus on my writing;

Barbara Battin, Barbara Kellett, Clem Nagel, Kyoko Katayama, and Lucy Hartwell,
who thoughtfully reviewed this manuscript;

and

all those with whom I have shared labyrinth pathways as we have prayed together.

The eleven-circuit Chartres labyrinth as documented by Robert Ferré

Introduction

What happens when a person walks the labyrinth over time?
Deeper connection with the sacred.
Creative surges.
Growing acceptance of others.
Joy!
Transformation.

How often should a person walk a labyrinth?
As often as one can!
Whenever one feels drawn to.

What is the best way to walk the labyrinth?
Any way one is ready to walk it.
With openness.

The labyrinth is an ancient sacred design equipped with a simple pathway leading to and from a center. Labyrinths have been used throughout history for varying purposes, including decoration, play, and prayer.
Although the path remains unchanged, no two experiences with a
labyrinth are the same.

Numerous approaches to labyrinth exploration are offered in this
book. It can be used by those who have never walked a labyrinth as
well as those who regularly use labyrinths. It is a book to be savored
over time. Each approach is self-contained; use the various ideas in any
order that makes sense for you. It is my hope that the suggestions on
the following pages will enhance your labyrinth experiences as well as
spark new ideas and walks for you. Feel free to adapt the exercises to
fit your needs.

The more a person explores the labyrinth, the more one comes to
appreciate the magnificent possibilities of this spiritual tool. May you
return again and again to the labyrinth and thereby discover its multi-
tudinous gifts.

Journeys to Creativity

The labyrinth pattern has one concentric, circular path
with no dead ends. Various styles of labyrinth patterns can be
found in ancient cultures from all over the world,
dating back as far as 5,000 years. These archetypal patterns
can be found in places as diverse as Peru, Arizona, Iceland,
Crete, Egypt, India, Sweden, England, and France.
Labyrinths find form in caves, rock patterns, etchings, stories,
and dance. In the past, labyrinths on the ground have been
used for ceremony and walking meditations.

—Barbara Kellett

1 · CREATIVE TRAVEL

Enter the labyrinth
as if you were crossing the border
into a country called Creativity.

In this land,
concepts of time and space
will hold different meanings
from those with which you are familiar.

While visiting,
experience the moment,
welcoming all gifts that are offered.

2 · LIGHTING THE WAY

Take a candle and matches
with you to the labyrinth.

Light the candle as you prepare for your walk.
Carry it symbolically with you
during your time in the labyrinth.

Use it to express your feelings,
thoughts,
and intuitions.

Afterwards,
reflect on the meanings of your experiences
through drawing,
playing a musical instrument,
journaling,
dancing,
or composing music.

3 · WHEN YOU HAVE TIME

Enter the labyrinth.

Whenever you feel you would like to take a moment to reflect,
to rest,
or to pray,
stop
and do so.

When you are ready,
continue on your way.

When you feel you would like to reflect,
or pray,
or rest more,
stop and do so.

Continue this process all the way in
and out of the labyrinth.

4 · STOKING THE FIRE

As you walk the labyrinth
pray the question,
"What fuels my spiritual passions?"

When you reach the center,
imagine that you are being warmed by divine fire.

Bask in the glow of the sacred experience.

At each turn
on your way out,
imagine that the coals of your burning passions
are being fanned into flames.

5 · GOING FOR A WALK

As you walk the labyrinth
remember other walks you have taken . . .
by the water,
with a friend or pet,
up a hill or mountain,
through the woods . . .

Wonder about how the walking you have done
relates to
the walking you are now doing
on the labyrinth.

The Sum Is More Than the Parts

The labyrinth is made of twelve concentric circles
enclosing eleven circuits. A single path leads a circuitous route
through the eleven circuits, turning seven times in each
quadrant plus six times at the entrance paths for a total of
thirty-four turns. The center contains six petals. There are ten
back-to-back turns, often called "labryses" because of their
resemblance to the double-headed ax of ancient Minoan culture.
The location of the labryses on the horizontal and vertical axes
gives a cruciform appearance to the labyrinth. Around the
perimeter are 113 lunations, so called because they form a lunar
calendar, used to determine the date of Easter.

— Robert Ferré

6 · WALKING INTO ANSWERS

At the threshold of the labyrinth
embrace the words,
"This is my opportunity."

Ask yourself,
"Do I have the courage to move on?"

Step into the answer.

7 · NEAR OR FAR?

Take notice:
when you first think you are close to the center of the labyrinth,
you are actually a long way from it.

However, when you seem far from the center,
you often discover that you arrive there quickly.

Walk the labyrinth
paying close attention
to your experience
of the center
and your perceptions of the distance between you and it.

8 · CLOSING A CIRCLE

As you grieve a recent loss . . .
as you anticipate the completion of an important project . . .
as you stand at any significant crossroads . . .
walk a labyrinth
as a symbolic act of honoring
what has been.

9 · INSIDE OUT

Walk directly to the center
from any point outside the labyrinth.
Do not follow the pathway to get there.

Pray, "I offer my going out to You,"
and follow the pathway away from the center
towards the threshold.

10 · TURNING

You make thirty-four turns on your way in
and again on your way out
of the labyrinth.

Before walking,
ask yourself and God:
"What can the turns
teach me today?"

Use each turn that you make
as an opportunity.

Hints:
Try different approaches such as
stopping,
twirling,
or stepping backwards into each turn.
If your hips start to hurt, slow down your turns.
If you begin to feel dizzy, stop and focus on an object in the distance.
Notice all sensations that occur.

11 · CIRCLING IN AND OUT

Study the pattern of the labyrinth.
Identify and count its circles.

As you enter the labyrinth
immediately turn to your right or left
and follow the circle all the way around.

(Don't pay attention to the turning of the path; walk right over the turns.)

When you have made a complete circle,
move in,
and walk all the way around the next circle.

When you finish,
move in,
and do the same with the next circle.

Keep moving inwards
until you are in the center.

When you are ready to leave the center,
reverse your process,
circling out,
one circle at a time.

12 · Circumambulating

Before entering
or after exiting the labyrinth
walk around its circumference.

Try walking clockwise,
noticing
sensations,
smells,
images,
intuitions,

sounds,
and thoughts
which accompany you.

Then try walking counterclockwise,
doing the same.

13 · CROSSING

As one studies labyrinths
one discovers that within them there lies a pattern
formed by the intersection of two perpendicular lines.

Instead of walking the pathway to the center and back out,
walk the cross.
Begin at the mouth, walking straight across the entire labyrinth to the
far side of it.
Then walk back to the center.
Next, walk out and back one of the "arms," returning to the center.
Finally, walk out and back the other arm, returning once again to
the center.

Ponder the learnings your body has perceived,
exploring the meanings of the cruciform which lies within the
labyrinth.

When you are ready,
either repeat the process
or walk out of the labyrinth on one of the four arms.

14 · HOLY MEANDERINGS

On a day when you are feeling playful,
imagine the labyrinth pathway
as a river of God's love
which is carrying you along its life-sustaining current.

Relax into the wonderful experience,
flowing to the center
and back to the threshold!

15 · WALKING OUTSIDE THE LINES

For a different experience of the labyrinth,
try walking
anywhere but on the path.

Learn everything you can
by exploring this sacred space
in all the ways that come to mind
and heart.

16 · BACK TO THE CENTER

Sometime you may find yourself
unexpectedly returning to the center.
This happens when you get turned around
after stepping off the path
or missing a turn.

Follow this path where it is leading you.

Back in the center,
be open
to what is there for you.

Now walk out
with gratitude
for having been given
a second opportunity
to be where you needed to be.

17 · THRESHOLD MOMENTS

As you anticipate
or are experiencing
a transition,
approach the labyrinth without entering it.

Stand or sit in front of the threshold.
Pray for wisdom.

Contemplating what is ahead
may be more valuable
than walking the path.

18 · WALKING THE LUNATIONS

Place your foot inside one of the one hundred thirteen lunations
found on the outer edge of the labyrinth.

Then place your other foot in the next one
... and the next
... and the next
... and the next.

Move all the way around the labyrinth in this way.
Learn about the lunations
through your feet and
the rest of your body.

PART 3

—✦—

Being with Others at the Labyrinth

My son Alexander walks with Amy and me
fairly regularly. Early on in our experience with the labyrinth,
he was five and a half. I asked him to be quiet as
we walked, to listen for the voice of God whispering to him. As
we walked, he asked me to carry him. At some point, I couldn't
keep quiet and asked him what he was thinking.
"Hush, I'm thinking," said Alexander. I walked through
another turn or two and again asked. Again he answered,
"Hush, I'm thinking." We walked some more, and I could not
keep quiet, "What are you thinking, Alexander?"
"I'm thinking this is like the voice of God. It starts in the center
of the world and goes out until everyone hears it."

—Battle A. Beasley, "A Labyrinth Journey"

19 · LOOKING IN THE MIRROR

While walking the labyrinth with others
—the larger the group the better—
try to perceive
a part of yourself
in each person.

Open your heart
to all those around you.

Pray for the well-being of each person.

Open your heart
to yourself.

Pray for yourself.

20 · PROCESSIONAL WALKING

Gather a group
to walk the labyrinth in procession.

Line up behind the threshold.

Have people enter the labyrinth one at a time,
leaving about three feet from one person to the next.

The first person should assume a deliberately slow pace,
walking the path to the center,
around the edge of each "petal,"

and out across the labryses
on the opposite side of the labyrinth from the threshold.
(Do not follow the pathway out.)

Have the group gather,
as soon as they process out,
at an agreed-upon location
to sing or pray together.

*This way of walking the labyrinth is believed to have medieval roots. Catechumens
at Chartres Cathedral in France would be baptized in a small chapel below the cathedral,
process up a stairway into the cathedral, walk all the way around the entire sanctuary, and
then enter the labyrinth. Upon reaching the center they would continue walking down the
central aisle to the high altar, where they would receive their first Eucharist.*

21 · SHARING THE SPACE

Walk the labyrinth at a time
when you know others also will be walking.

Ask yourself and God:
"What can I learn
by paying attention to the other people
who are walking here with me?"

22 · INTERCEDING FOR OTHERS

Bring into your consciousness
people for whom you would like to pray.

At the mouth of the labyrinth
name them,
one by one,
placing their needs into divine care.

Walk the labyrinth
paying attention to
the longings on their behalf
which fill your heart.

Notice how your understandings,
hopes,
and feelings
shift and develop.

When you return to the mouth of the labyrinth,
name them once more.

Express your gratitude for divine care.

23 · SEEING DEEPLY

Find a comfortable place close to a labyrinth.

Witness those on the labyrinth
with an attitude of openness
and deep respect.

Receive the gifts which come
in the form of thoughts,
impressions,
feelings,
and images.

24 · A NEW CONTEXT FOR AN ESTABLISHED GROUP

Take a group with whom you study or pray
to the labyrinth.

Walk in together holding hands
as you follow the pathway.

Use your time in the center
to celebrate the meanings of your work together.
This can be done verbally or nonverbally.

Join hands once again
before walking out.

25 · FOLLOWING AND LEADING

Arrange to meet a friend at a labyrinth.

Before beginning,
decide who will walk in to the center first.
Let that person enter the labyrinth;
the second person is to follow closely behind.
The "leader" will determine the pace of the walk for both people.

Spend as much time in the center as feels right.
Do not talk to each other.

On the way out of the center,
whoever entered second will leave first,
moving as feels right;
the other person is to follow closely behind,
mirroring the leader's pace.

After exiting the labyrinth
spend time talking about the experiences and perceptions
you and your friend have just had.

If you have time,
walk the labyrinth again,
reversing the entire process.

26 · PERFECT PHOTO OPPORTUNITIES

Take with you to the labyrinth
a photo of someone you want to pray for.

On the way to the center
let your prayer for this person
be a gentle gazing at her or his image.

Place the photo in the center of the labyrinth
when you get there.
Stand or sit nearby reflecting on the person in the picture—
his or her life, needs, and relationships.

When you are ready,
pick up the photograph.
Determine how you would like to walk out with it.
You may wish to continue the meditative gazing you did on the way in,
or to put the photo in a pocket and simply walk with remembrance,
or to carry on a conversation with God about the person
as you occasionally glance at the picture.

Before leaving the labyrinth
give thanks for this experience
and for the person whose image
has accompanied you.

27 · INTRODUCING ONE FRIEND TO ANOTHER

One day you might think,
"I know who would really enjoy walking a labyrinth!"
It is a realization that has come to countless labyrinth walkers
before you.

Wait until the time feels right
and then invite your friend to go walk a labyrinth with you.

When you get there,
explain that there are as many ways to walk the labyrinth
as there are people who walk it.
Mention that there is only one pathway in and out;
no one gets lost although sometimes people get turned around.
Say anything else that you think will help your friend
relax and enjoy the experience.

Then ask, "Would you like me to go in first, or would you like to?"
Note that if your paces differ, each of you should feel free to go around
the other.
Before the first person begins, agree on a place to meet when you are
both finished.
Assure your friend, "Take as much time as you would like."

Be open to talking about the experience afterwards.
Realize that it might be too soon
for your friend to verbalize or share any response.

28 · DIFFERING PERCEPTIONS

Go to the labyrinth with a friend.
Bring a blindfold.

Have your friend lead you
with your eyes covered
in and out of the labyrinth.

As you cross the threshold
do not remove the blindfold
until after you have discussed
your experiences with each other.

If it feels right
blindfold your friend
and repeat the process.

29 · RECONNECTING

A labyrinth is the kind of place
where connecting with memories
of deceased friends and family members
is both possible
and fruitful.

As you walk the labyrinth
open your heart and mind
to memories of a person who has died.

Receive
the gifts that come.
They are an expression
of divine love
for you.

PART 4

✦

This Could Happen to You

But the oldest practice is still the best.
Take your soul for a stroll. Long walks, short walks,
morning walks, evening walks—whatever form or length it
takes. Walking is the best way to get out of your head.
Recall the invocation of the philosopher Søren Kierkegaard,
who said, "Above all, do not lose your desire to walk:
Every day I walk myself into a state of well-being and
walk away from every illness; I have walked myself
into my best thoughts."

—Phil Cousineau, *The Art of Pilgrimage:
The Seeker's Guide to Making Travel Sacred*

30 · Going Back . . . to Go Forward

On a walk you may discover
that even though you left the threshold
on your way "in"
you may arrive back there
before getting to the center.

Or, on the way "out,"
that you have gotten turned around
and returned to the center!

If this happens,
you can either "begin again" from the center or threshold,
or you can decide that your walk is complete.

Either way,
be sure to ask yourself,
"Is there anything I can glean from this experience
of arriving somewhere I thought I had left behind?"

31 · Interrupting the Flow

Sooner or later
while you are walking the labyrinth
something or someone will catch your attention
and you will want to interrupt your walk.

Mark your spot,
mentally or physically.
Be sure to note which direction you were facing.

Go attend to whatever draws you.

When you are able,
come back and resume your labyrinth walk.

In the center,
or after you are finished walking,
reflect upon how interruptions affect you.

32 · ONE STEP AT A TIME

As you pray the labyrinth
notice your pace.

Repeat the phrase
"One step at a time"
as you walk.

Pay attention
to any phrases that pop into your mind.
If one comes, begin repeating it.

If another comes,
shift, and repeat that one.

Otherwise,
continue repeating, "One step at a time."

Imagine that each phrase you say
is a stepping-stone
and that you are walking across these stones
toward . . .

Accept the mystery of your destination
while enjoying the moment at hand.

33 · BEFORE OR AFTER A FUNERAL

When you are grieving,
go to a labyrinth.

Imagine the person you are missing
in the center of God's love.

As you move towards,
then away
from the center of the labyrinth,
be aware of any feelings of connectedness
and disconnectedness
with the person
and God.

P A R T   5

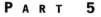

Embodied Explorations

Many people are surprised by the instant rapport
they feel with a labyrinth. Its basic circularity incorporates a
universal shape reflected throughout nature and the solar system.
Three-dimensionally, the circle becomes a sphere, the shape
of atoms, the earth, the sun, planets, and stars. The circle is in us,
and we are in it. We are made of circles.

—Robert Ferré, *The Labyrinth Revival*

34 · CLAP YOUR HANDS

As you walk the labyrinth
begin clapping your hands.

Clap according to rhythms
that emerge from within.

Allow your clapping to shift naturally.

With your hands
leading you,
allow other parts of yourself
to follow expressively.

35 · RESTRICTING AND FREEING YOURSELF

Tie a piece of cloth or a scarf
loosely around both your ankles
or another part of your body you usually use freely.

Then move towards the center of the labyrinth,
noticing the sensations,
emotions,
and thoughts
that accompany you.

When you feel ready,
take off the cloth or scarf
and walk the rest of the labyrinth

without the encumbrance,
exploring any changes in sensations,
emotions,
and thoughts.

36 · INTERNAL LABYRINTHS

Walk to the center.

From the inside of the labyrinth
ponder the truth
that you have many labyrinths in your own body.
There are two located inside your ears.
Others are suggested by the shape of your fingerprints.
Your brain,
lungs,
heart,
and digestive system
all have labyrinthine qualities.

As you walk out
ask yourself,
"What did I know or understand about labyrinths
before I ever walked one?"

37 · CLOSE YOUR EYES

Find out what happens
if you try to walk the labyrinth
with your eyes shut.

If you are walking on a canvas labyrinth,
take off your shoes and socks.
As you slowly proceed,
try to perceive the edges of the path.

If you are walking on a labyrinth with grass
or other natural path markers,
use them as your guides.

What you learn about how you proceed
may be more important than arriving at your destination!

38 · FOLLOWING SACRED NUDGINGS

Consider a labyrinth walker's journal entry:
"I notice that so much of what I feel led to do as I walk the labyrinth
doesn't register with my conscious mind.
It doesn't make mental 'sense.'
Yet when I respond to ideas which feel like invitations—
walk backwards,
play with turning,
step off the labyrinth—
shifts seem to occur deep within.
Even though words and images do not accompany me at such times,
transformation does!"

At the mouth of the labyrinth,
ask for sensitivity and courage
to respond to divine leadings.

Enter the labyrinth.
As ideas,
impressions,
and invitations
present themselves to you,
express them with your body.

39 · PAYING ATTENTION TO YOUR BODY

Physical changes may occur
while walking a labyrinth.

Some discover that there is a significant difference in their heart rate
before and after walking the labyrinth.

Those aware of breathing techniques notice
using both nostrils simultaneously.

Others speak of a sense of embodied peacefulness.

Before walking the labyrinth
make mental or physical notes
about your experience of your body.

Walk the labyrinth,
alert to any bodily shifts you experience.

After leaving the labyrinth
make mental or written notes about your body,
including observations about any physical changes.

40 · BE A SNAIL

When you have at least an hour,
enter the labyrinth.

Place each foot on the path of the labyrinth
carefully.

Notice what you are learning
as you take time on the path.

Use a deliberate pace all the way in
and out.

41 · WHY NOT PLAY ON THE LABYRINTH?!

What does it feel like to skip the pathway
all the way to the center?

Chase a friend in or out.

Experiment with an occasional somersault
or cartwheel on the path.

Can you rollerblade the labyrinth?

Be as creative and playful as you can imagine.

Enjoy the labyrinth!

42 · WHAT WOULD HAPPEN . . .

if
you did
exactly what your body wanted to
as you moved on the labyrinth?

Try it!

Find out!

43 · KNOWING FEET

At the mouth of the labyrinth
take off your shoes and socks.
Look at your bare feet.

Look again,
noticing what appears most beautiful about them.
Place your hands on your feet
and bless them with a prayer.

Consciously decide to walk the labyrinth
as if all you could know
came from what your feet experienced
and communicated.

As you walk on the path
learn from the experience
of your feet praying for you.

When your walk is finished
look at your bare feet.
Look again,
noticing what appears most beautiful about them.
Place your hands on your feet and bless them.

44 · BACKING AWAY/TOWARDS

Spend some time during your labyrinth walk
proceeding backwards.

You may want to back your way to the center.

Or you may choose to walk in forwards
and walk out backwards.

Perhaps you will sense your best approach
is to walk to a turn,
and then back up to the next one,
repeating this pattern of walking ahead,
backing ahead.

Or create a different pattern of forwards/backwards moving.

Explore:
What am I observing about my balance,
preferences,
and emotions?

What am I learning about my approaches to life?

45 · MOVING

When faced with a literal or figurative move
(from one location to another
or from one approach to life to another),
walk the labyrinth
praying,
"How will I move?"

Be aware of the physical messages
your body communicates.

Consider how the way you are walking
mirrors what is happening in your life.

Are you proceeding quickly or dragging your feet?

Are you moving peacefully or with a lot of anxiety?

46 · Do You Want to Dance?

As you prepare to traverse the labyrinth
ask yourself,
"What would my experience of the labyrinth be
if I danced the path
instead of walked it?"

Dance your way to the center
and back out.

47 · Pacing Yourself

When things are not moving along as you would like in life,
walk the labyrinth
experimenting with your pace.
Feel free to move around others as you need to.

Walk quickly,
noticing the varying responses
of your body and mind.

Slow down,
paying attention to your breathing and thoughts.

Speed up, or walk more leisurely,
depending on what you are discovering.

Keep varying your rate
as you become aware

of how and what
your body is teaching you.

Rest
in the center.

Walk out using the pace that feels just right
for the moment.

48 · FOLLOWING ANCIENT PILGRIMS

It is said that medieval pilgrims prayed the labyrinth on their knees.

Try it.
Knee pads might be a good idea.

49 · MEMORIAL DAY

When you want to remember those who have died,
take a bell, drum, flute, whistle, rain stick, wind chime, or other instrument
with you to the labyrinth.

Walk to the center,
carrying your memories of those deceased.

In the center
play the instrument in memory of the dead.

Follow your heart's leading,
moving the instrument and your body
in ways that express what you are thinking and feeling
as you walk out.

50 · ZEROING IN

As you walk the labyrinth
pay attention to everything
inside and outside of you.

Notice things like
the temperature,
who else is around,
the sounds you hear,
what you can see,
the smells that capture your attention,
and your feelings.

When you have done this,
choose one image,
emotion,
sensation,
scent,
or sound,
and focus your attention on it exclusively as you walk.

Let this intense awareness
be your companion.

PART 6

*Intentional Encounters
with the Divine*

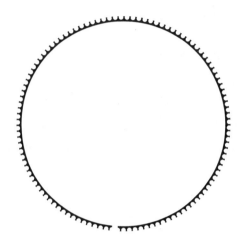

If you want to get to know God better, take a walk with God.

— Asa, four years old

51 · BEING DRAWN IN

Stand at the threshold of the labyrinth.
Imagine that a magnet is lodged in the middle of your breastbone.

As you walk the labyrinth
feel yourself being pulled
towards the center.

When you arrive at the center
ask the Divine,
"Why have you drawn me here?"

52 · MOVING WITH YOUR CENTER

As you prepare to walk the labyrinth
pray the question,
"What is my Center?"

Consider the meanings of moving towards your Center—
emotionally,
spiritually,
physically—
as you move towards the center of the labyrinth.

In its center
explore your Center.

As you physically move away from the center of the labyrinth,
pray the question,
"How do I stay attuned to my Center?"

53 · NESTING

Walk to the center of the labyrinth.

Imagine you are a baby bird
and the labyrinth is your home.

Ponder,
"In what ways do I experience and know God
in this nest?"

54 · THANKS GIVING

Find a way—
or many ways—
to express your gratitude
as you walk the labyrinth.

55 · YOUR OFFERING

At the threshold pray,
"I offer to you . . ."
(complete the sentence in a way that feels right
and makes sense to you).

Walk the labyrinth
repeating this phrase over and over.
Pay attention to images,

feelings,
sensations,
and thoughts
that surface.

When your walk is complete
once again pray,
"I offer to you . . ."

56 · COMMUNICATING WITH YOUR BODY

Imagine
that God only perceives communication
expressed through bodily movements and motions.

Use your labyrinth walk
as a time to converse with the Divine
using your various muscles,
but no words.

57 · LETTING GO

Walk towards the center
with the intention of releasing something.

When you sense you might be ready,
shake it out,
drop it,
or release it in any other way that feels right.

If you still have it when you get to the center,
offer it to God.

As you move out,
do not take it with you.

As needed,
ask God for the resolve
to resist any impulse to go back
and retrieve it.

As you cross the threshold of the labyrinth,
give thanks for your willingness to leave it there with God.

58 · Surprise Rendezvous

Your Beloved
is waiting for you
as you cross the threshold into the labyrinth.

Spend time
communing deeply.

Express
whatever you have been hoping to communicate.

Receive every expression of love
that is offered.

59 · SACRED OFFERINGS

To seek divine blessing
on a gift you wish to share with the world,
bring it
(or a representation of it)
to the labyrinth.

At the threshold
and as you walk the labyrinth
seek God's blessing
on this gift
using movements
and words that emerge.

60 · WORSHIPING

Worship
the Divine
during your entire walk.

Use words,
gestures,
songs,
movements,
or ancient prayers.

PART 7

✦

Experiencing Outdoor Labyrinths

The California Pacific Medical Center, an acute-care
hospital in San Francisco, unveiled a painted labyrinth outside the
entrance that is now walked by emergency room nurses as well
as surgery patients and their families. . . .

On sunny days, Dr. Martin Brotman [president and chief
executive of California Pacific] says he finds patients in bathrobes
plodding along the labyrinth's twisting path. Families spot it from
their chairs in the waiting room and are invited to try it.

"What are their choices," Dr. Brotman asked, "to sit and worry,
watch TV, try to read a book—which is unsuccessful—or to give
themselves a little mental relaxation and walk the labyrinth?"

—Laurie Goodstein, "Reviving Labyrinths,
Paths to Inner Peace"

61 · MOON GAZING

When the moon is visible
walk an outdoor Chartres-style labyrinth
with lunations.

Watch the moon
as you walk in.

In the center
wonder about possible relationships
between the moon and the labyrinth.

Receive the blessings
of light and energy
from above
and below
as you walk out.

62 · WHISPERED TRUTHS

As you walk an outdoor labyrinth
pay close attention to how your body feels the wind
that is there with you.

Somewhere along your way
wonder,
"What is the wind communicating?"

If its messages
require a response,
respond!

63 · AWESOME WONDERING

Go to an outdoor labyrinth on a starry night.

Walk until you find a spot which invites you to stay.
Or walk to the center.

Get as comfortable as you can.
Gaze at the incredible sky with openness.
The best way to do this may be lying on your back!

When you must,
leave the labyrinth.

Take your experiences of awe with you!

64 · REACHING IN AND OUT

Even as the labyrinth naturally takes you inward,
stay tuned in to your external surroundings.

As you wind your way towards the center
and away from it,
use your senses
as springboards for prayer.

When sounds arrive at the labyrinth
pray for children you hear playing,
the police whose siren is shrieking,
or the workers building noisily in the area.

As your eyes take in the people, buildings, and landscape surrounding you,
intercede for all you see,
asking for God's blessings to be realized.

Let the ground you feel below your feet,
the air which caresses your skin,
the smells which waft past,
or the squeeze of your hand offered by another walker on the path
inspire your prayers.

PART 8

Opening to Wisdom

The [one] who reaches the centre of the labyrinth,
having made the ritual progress through it and having "danced,"
is changed and for all I know in the sense that there has
been an opening of the intuition to natural laws and harmonies;
to laws and harmonies that [s]he will perhaps not understand but
which [s]he will experience in [her]himself, with which [s]he
will feel in tune and which will be for [her]him the best test
of truth as the diapason is the "test" for a musician.

—Louis Charpentier, *The Mysteries of the Chartres Cathedral*

65 · PRAYING A QUESTION

Ask a question
at the mouth of the labyrinth.

Ask it out loud
if you feel comfortable doing so.

Write it down
if it helps to see it.

Hear it internally
as you consider it.

Share it with the Divine.

Walk the labyrinth
open to receive whatever comes.

Welcome the ways that the question may change as you walk.
Note new ideas, memories, and images that present themselves.

Make mental or physical notes
of all that you have experienced
before leaving.

66 · REMEMBERING

Identify a memory
that you would like to explore with God.

Imagine the memory
as a tight bud of a morning glory,
and the labyrinth as the sun
which will gently warm and open it.

Ask for the watering Spirit of God
to flow through you,
instilling new life.

Walk the labyrinth with the memory.

Welcome what comes,
allowing your perceptions of the memory
to be transformed.

67 · JOURNALING ALL THE WAY

Take your journal with you as you walk the labyrinth.

Whenever something comes into your consciousness—
a sensation,
thought,
song,
movement,
image,
scent,

question,
or something else—
document it.

Keep moving,
keep documenting
all the way in,
in the center,
and all the way out.

When your walk is complete,
close your journal.

Plan a time in the future
when you will return to reflect on
the record of these experiences.

68 · REWORKING AND REJOICING

Focus on something which is important to you,
yet incomplete—
a poem or sketch you've been working on,
a thought that is troubling you,
a dance you are creating,
your response to a quotation whose deepest meanings elude you.

Take this with you to the labyrinth.

Before entering,
ask God to be present,
revealing new possibilities.

Walk in,
spend time in the center,
and walk out,
stopping whenever it seems time to explore,
revise,
or create.

Do so,
rejoicing in the opening
you experience.

69 · ROLE PLAYING

Identify one of the roles you assume
(parent or child, employee, friend, volunteer, etc.).

As you enter the labyrinth
feel yourself taking on that role
and letting all other roles go.

Walk in character
sensing the many meanings and expressions
of the role you are exploring.

In the center
open yourself to divine input
concerning your embodiment
of this role.

On the way out
imagine new expressions

of the role.
Feel free to experiment.

As you cross the threshold
let your inspirations
lead you.

70 · SPIRITUAL TRAVELING COMPANIONS

Take one of your spiritual tools—
a musical instrument,
a spiritual image or icon,
your Scriptures,
a prayer—
to the labyrinth.

Welcome the intuitions
that suggest what you are to do
as you walk.

Act on them.

71 · WALKING A QUESTION THROUGH THE FOUR SEASONS

Take a question you wish to explore
with you to the labyrinth.

As you stand at the threshold
mentally divide the labyrinth into four quadrants.
Assign each section one of the four seasons.

As you walk through a quadrant
imagine what it would feel like to ask your question
in the season it represents.

Be prepared to wind in and out of each season many times
as you follow the path in and out.

72 · HAPPY BIRTHDAY

In honor of the day that you were born,
and in honor of your life,
walk the labyrinth on your birthday.

Reflect on the year that has just passed,
and dream about the year that is to come.

Ask the questions
that need to be asked.

Pray the prayers
that are in your heart.

73 · SHEDDING

Like a snake
shedding its skin as it grows,
walk the labyrinth
when it is time to let go of something.

As you walk to the center
imagine your old skin dropping away.

In the center
welcome sensations of renewal and growth.

As you walk out
become aware of your expanding reality.

After crossing the threshold
give thanks
for what has been,
what is,
and what will be.

PART 9

Biblical Meditations for Labyrinth Praying

You show me the path of life.
In your presence there is fullness of joy;
in your right hand are pleasures forevermore.

—Psalm 16:11

74 · EXPLORING THE VALLEY OF THE SHADOW OF DEATH
   Psalm 23:4

Read Psalm 23 (King James Version).
When you are done, return to verse 4:
"Yea, though I walk through the valley of the shadow of death,
I will fear no evil,
for thou art with me; thy rod and thy staff, they comfort me."

Walk to the center of the labyrinth
imagining that it is the valley of the shadow of death.

Notice the feelings,
thoughts,
memories,
and sensations
that accompany you.

In the center
rest in God's presence.
Communicate with God
about what it is like to walk through the shadows.

On the way out
reenter the shadows
with the awareness
of what God communicated with you.

75 · PRAYING THE LORD'S PRAYER
Matthew 6:9–13

Recite the Lord's Prayer
using a version that you like
as you walk the labyrinth.
Pray then in this way:
"Our Father/Mother in heaven,
hallowed be your name.
Your kindom come.
Your will be done, on earth as it is in heaven.
Give us this day our daily bread.
And forgive us our debts, as we also have forgiven our debtors.
And do not bring us to the time of trial, but rescue us from evil."

Notice the relationship of
your moving body
and the words of the ancient prayer.

76 · GROUNDED, ROOTED, AND GROWING
Jeremiah 17:7–8

Walk to the center of the labyrinth.

Prayerfully consider the words of Jeremiah:
"Blessed are those who trust in God,
whose trust is God.
They shall be like a tree planted by water,
sending out its roots by the stream.

It shall not fear when heat comes,
and its leaves shall stay green;
in the year of drought it is not anxious,
and it does not cease to bear fruit."

Stand in the center of the labyrinth.
Allow your feet to feel strongly rooted in the Divine.
Imagine yourself or your spiritual community as that tree.
Welcome the images and wisdom that come.

77 · Praying for Someone in Need

Ephesians 6:18

"Pray at all times in the Spirit,
with all prayer and supplication.
To that end keep alert with all perseverance,
making supplication for all the saints."

As you prepare to walk the labyrinth
communicate with God
about a person who has a special need.

Decide on a simple prayer phrase for that person
that you can repeat verbally or silently
as you walk.

Stay aware of any images,
words,
or thoughts
which come as you pray your way through the labyrinth.

After leaving the labyrinth,
write a note to the person for whom you have prayed.

78 · RESTING

Matthew 11:28

Walk on the labyrinth
until you come to a place that feels really peaceful.
Be assured that this place is waiting for you.

Once there, get as comfortable as you can.
Remember, others can walk around you if they need to!

Recall Jesus' words as recorded in Matthew 11:28,
"Come to me, all who labor and are heavy laden, and I will give you rest."

Imagine God saying to you,
"[Your name], rest in me.
Rest with me.
Rest,
there is time."

Breathe deeply from your diaphragm.
Ask your body to relax more fully.

Enjoy any and all experiences of rest that follow.

When you are done resting,
continue your walk.

79 · THANKSGIVING

Psalm 9:1–2

Go to the labyrinth
with the sole purpose of expressing gratitude to the Divine.

As you prepare to walk, consider:
"I will give thanks to God with my whole heart;
I will tell of all your wonderful deeds.
I will be glad and exult in you;
I will sing praise to your name."

Walk the labyrinth out of thankfulness.
Do so silently,
or verbalize all that you want to say or sing.

If your attention wanders from your experience of gratitude,
bring it back.
Focus your entire walk on those feelings,
memories,
and thoughts
which inspire thankfulness.

As you leave the labyrinth
find an embodied way to express your gratefulness.

80 · THE WIDE OPEN PATH
   2 Samuel 22:33

While following the labyrinth pathway,
explore the possible meanings of
"The God who has girded me with strength
has opened wide my path."

81 · A MIND TO UNDERSTAND, EYES TO SEE, EARS TO HEAR
   Deuteronomy 29:2–4

Contemplate the contemporary meanings of these verses from
Deuteronomy:

"Moses summoned all Israel and said to them: You have seen all that
God did before your eyes in the land of Egypt, to Pharaoh and to all his
servants and to all his land, the great trials that your eyes saw, the signs,
and those great wonders.
But to this day God has not given you a mind to understand, or eyes to
see, or ears to hear."

Pray at the mouth of the labyrinth:
"What are You inviting me to
understand,
see,
and hear?"

Pray in the center of the labyrinth:
"What are You inviting me to
understand,

see,
and hear?"

Pray as you leave the labyrinth:
"What are You inviting me to
understand,
see,
and hear?"

82 · REFRESHMENT
Revelation 21:5–6

Before walking,
read Revelation 21:5–6:
"See, I am making all things new . . .
I am the Alpha and the Omega, the beginning and the end.
To the thirsty I will give water as a gift from the spring of the
water of life."

Imagine a strong spring bubbling up from the earth
in the center of the labyrinth.

As you walk toward the spring
experience your thirsts—
physical,
spiritual,
emotional.

When you arrive at the center,
drink
whatever divine gifts are offered you.

Return to the mouth of the labyrinth
gratefully conscious
of the spring that remains in the center.

83 · YOUR WILL BE DONE
Matthew 6:10

Approach the labyrinth
when seeking guidance relating to
a perplexing question,
situation,
or relationship.

Pray,
"Your will be done,"
as you walk in
and out of the labyrinth.

Pray it once at the threshold,
repeatedly as you walk,
or as a refrain
to other more personalized prayers.

84 · THE FRUIT OF WALKING THE LABYRINTH
Galatians 5:22–23

Walk the labyrinth
reflecting on the ways
that labyrinth praying
is part of the ripening
going on in your life.

In the center
reflect on Galatians 5:22–23:
"The fruit of the Spirit is
love,
joy,
peace,
patience,
kindness,
generosity,
faithfulness,
gentleness, and
self-control."

Walk out expressing gratitude
for deepening embodiment of Spirit.

85 · AN OASIS IN THE DESERT

Psalm 107:35

On a day when you are feeling depleted,
approach the labyrinth
as a desert traveler draws near to an oasis.

At the threshold
consider Psalm 107:35:
"God turns a desert into pools of water,
a parched land into springs of water."

Enter
with anticipation of refreshment and renewal.

Drink deeply
of the waters of the labyrinth.

86 · SACRED FORMATION

Isaiah 44:2

"Thus says [God] who made you,
who formed you in the womb
and will help you:
Do not fear."

Envision the labyrinth
as a womb
in which you are developing.

Move around freely
exploring the territory.

87 · LIKE A LITTLE CHILD

Mark 10:13–16

"People were bringing little children to Jesus in order that Jesus might touch them; and the disciples spoke sternly to them. But when Jesus saw this, Jesus was indignant and said to them, 'Let the little children come to me; do not stop them; for it is to such as these that the kingdom of God belongs. Truly I tell you, whoever does not receive the kingdom of God as a little child will never enter it.' And Jesus took them up in his arms, laid his hands on them, and blessed them."

Take a young friend with you to the labyrinth.

Let the child explore it,
run it,
play on it,
and do whatever else comes to mind
and body.

As you share this amazing experience
give yourself permission
to enjoy the labyrinth
as much as your young friend.

At the right time,
now or later,
reflect on how Jesus' teaching in Mark 10:13–16
may relate to the time the two of you spent at the labyrinth.

✥

Let Your Fingers Do the Walking

The labyrinth is truly a tool for our times. It can help
us find our way through the bewildering multiplicity, to the unity
of source. The labyrinth is an evocative experience.
The labyrinth provides the sacred space where the inner and
outer worlds can commune, where the thinking mind and
imaginative heart can flow together. It can provide a
space to listen to our inner voice of wisdom and come to grips
with our role in humankind's next evolutionary step.
Troubled communities can come to the labyrinth to discover
and synchronize their vision. It gives us a glimpse of
other realms and other ways of knowing.

—Lauren Artress, *Walking a Sacred Path:
Rediscovering the Labyrinth as a Spiritual Tool*

88 · WALKING THE LABYRINTH BY HAND

Use your finger or a pen to follow the pathway from the entrance in to the center and back out. Notice what you perceive as you experience the labyrinth in this way.

89 · BEING ROCKED

Parents comfort children by rocking them gently.

As your finger enters the labyrinth
pay attention to the back-and-forth motion of your hand on the path.

If your finger labyrinth allows,
close your eyes and feel the gentle rocking motion.

Sense the ways in which your body is comforted
by the movement within the labyrinth.

When you reach the center
rest.

When you are ready to be comforted on a deeper level,
let your finger enter the pathway heading out.
Slowly let it make its way
back and forth,
back and forth,
back and forth.

Welcome body and mental memories of rocking
and physical comfort.

90 · FINGERING

Follow the pathway of the labyrinth
with each of your fingers on the hand you use most naturally.

Then follow the pathway
with each of the fingers on the other hand.

If your finger labyrinth is grooved,
and you would like to heighten your awareness,
close your eyes,
feeling your way through the labyrinth with your fingertips.

91 · COLORING

Using crayons, markers, or colored pencils,
color a paper labyrinth.
Do not feel any compulsion to stay within the lines!

Take as much time as you need,
using as many colors as you desire.

Use the custom-designed labyrinth
as a visual aid for prayer,
or in any other way your creativity suggests.

PART 11

Try This!

[The one] who ventures courageously into a labyrinth seeking to
find the truth of [her]his life is forced by its circuitous pathways to
circumambulate the center of [her]himself, to learn to relate with
it and to perceive it from all sides.

—Helmut Jaskolski, *The Labyrinth:*
Symbol of Fear, Rebirth, and Liberation

92 · When Upset

If it seems very difficult to disconnect
from troubling thoughts,
go to a labyrinth
and pray.

Let the movements of your body
and the winding pathway
help you to find peace.

Keep walking until your mind quiets.
It may take two or three or even four walks to the center and back out.

As you finish your labyrinth experience,
give thanks
for where your walk has brought you.

93 · Walking and Resting

Walk the labyrinth pathway to the center.

Assume a posture that feels relaxing.
(I like to lie down; some like to sit or stand!)

Rest for at least five minutes.
Twenty minutes is much more beneficial.

Relish each moment of relaxation.
Enjoy the feelings of renewal which come.

When you are ready,
walk the labyrinth path out.

94 · GAINING KNOWLEDGE, GAINING WISDOM

Read a book or article about the labyrinth
(many excellent ones are listed in the bibliography).
Consider what you have learned.

Walk a labyrinth.
Notice what you have learned.

Complete the following sentences as many times as you can:
Intellectual knowledge tells me . . .
Body wisdom tells me . . .
Intellectual knowledge tells me . . .
Body wisdom tells me . . .
Intellectual knowledge tells me . . .
Body wisdom tells me . . .

When you can't think of any more responses,
reflect on your answers.
Pay attention to ways in which the two learning styles complement
each other.

95 · WORKING WITH A DREAM

After having a dream you would like to explore more fully,
go to a labyrinth.

Recall the dream or dream fragment.

Ask for divine help.

"God,
I bring my dream with me
to the labyrinth.

I ask for:
insight,
clarity,
healing,
and whatever else you want to gift me with.

Amen."

Walk the labyrinth,
open to receiving insights,
images,
and understandings
that present themselves.

96 · TUNING IN

Choose a song,
hymn,
or tune
which is particularly meaningful to you.

Sing it or hum it over and over
as you walk the labyrinth.

Let it
inform
and shape
your reality.

97 · BEING HERE

Before entering the labyrinth
consider labyrinth maker Robert Ferré's comment:
"The labyrinth works on so many levels
that it meets us where we are."

At the mouth of the labyrinth ask,
"Where am I?"

Enter with the expectation of discovering more!

98 · SPIRITUAL EXPLORING

What about combining your labyrinth walk
with another of your spiritual practices?

Stop somewhere on the labyrinth
and meditate.

Meet a friend in the center,
join hands and pray together silently or verbally.

Take your scriptures with you.
Read them devotionally
when the time and place feel right.

Use the center as a space to do tai chi
or a yoga pose that is longing to be explored there.

Repeat a favorite mantra
as your walking companion.

Chant
your way in and back out.

99 · SWEEP YOUR WAY TO THE CENTER

Take a broom with you to a canvas labyrinth,
or a rake with you to an outdoor one.

Sweep or rake all the way to the center
and back out.
Expect this process to take a while!

Allow your movements to inspire your prayer.

100 · COMING TOGETHER

Approach the labyrinth
as you would an old friend
who has been waiting patiently
for your arrival.

Discover what happens
while you spend time together.

101 · CARING

Go to the labyrinth that you walk most often.

Sit beside the labyrinth
or walk around it
considering what care it may need now
or in the future.

As you pay attention to feelings of gratitude,
commit yourself to a practical act of caring
for the labyrinth,
such as cleaning its surface
or building a bench to put nearby.

Labyrinth Resources

Caerdroia
53 Thundersley Grove
Thundersley, Essex SS7 3EB, England
Telephone: 01268751915
Jeff Saward, editor
Caerdroia@dial.pipex.com
Written resources and annual publication

The Labyrinth Society
www.labyrinthsociety.org

The Saint Louis Labyrinth Project
Robert Ferré
128 Slocum
St. Louis, MO 63119-2254
1-800-873-9873; fax 1-888-873-9873
www.1heart.com or robert@1heart.com
Written resources, labyrinth travel, labyrinth construction consultations

Veriditas: The World-Wide Labyrinth Project
Grace Cathedral
1100 California Street
San Francisco, CA 94108-9858
415-749-6358; fax 415-749-6357
www.gracecom.org
Labyrinth products, including 36-foot portable canvas labyrinths.
Use their on-line labyrinth locator to find local and distant labyrinths.

Wisdom Ways Resource Center for Spirituality
1890 Randolph Avenue
St. Paul, MN 55105
651-690-8830; fax 651-696-2771
Laminated 12-inch paperboard finger labyrinths (the reverse side
includes a brief history of the labyrinth and suggestions for preparing
to walk the labyrinth)

Bibliography

Artress, Lauren. *Walking a Sacred Path: Rediscovering the Labyrinth as a Spiritual Tool.* New York: Riverhead Books, 1995.

Beasley, Battle A. "A Labyrinth Journey." *The Source: A Veriditas Publication* 5 (fall 1997): 7.

Bord, Janet. *Mazes and Labyrinths of the World.* New York: E. P. Dutton, 1976.

Bourgeois, Jean-Louis. "Surprise! The Seven-Circuit Labyrinth, Chartres, and the Harmonists." *Labyrinth Letter* 3, no. 4 (October 1997): 4–8.

Cain, Marty. "Tools for Life: A Search." *Labyrinth Letter* 1, no. 1 (April 1995): 12–14.

Campbell, Scott. "Mazes and Labyrinths: A Search for the Center." Scottsdale, Ariz.: Lutz Limited, 1996.

Champion, Alex. "A Labyrinth Is a Type of Maze." *Caerdroia* 28 (1997): 35–42.

Charpentier, Louis. *The Mysteries of the Chartres Cathedral.* Haverhill, Eng.: Rilko Books, 1960.

Coffey, Kathy. "Labyrinth Prayer." *Praying* 64 (January–February 1995): 20.

Cousineau, Phil. *The Art of Pilgrimage: The Seeker's Guide to Making Travel Sacred.* Berkeley, Calif.: Conari Press, 1998.

Fairchild, Kristen. "Veriditas and the Worldwide Labyrinth Project." <http://www.gracecom.org/veriditas/features/vision.shtml> (1997): 1–16.

Ferré, Robert. "Constructing Labyrinths." St. Louis: The St. Louis Labyrinth Project, 1998.

———. "How to Make a Masking Tape Labyrinth." St. Louis: The St. Louis Labyrinth Project, 1997.

———. *The Labyrinth Revival.* St. Louis: One Way Press, 1996.

Geoffrion, Jill Kimberly Hartwell. *Praying the Labyrinth: A Journal for Spiritual Exploration.* Cleveland: The Pilgrim Press, 1999.

Goodstein, Laurie. "Reviving Labyrinths, Paths to Inner Peace." *New York Times,* 10 May 1998, 20.

Jaskolski, Helmut. *The Labyrinth: Symbol of Fear, Rebirth, and Liberation.* Trans. Michael H. Kohn. Boston: Shambhala, 1997.

Kellett, Barbara. Paper prepared for Wisdom Ways Resource Center for Spirituality Labyrinth Dedication, St. Paul, Minn., fall 1998.

Ketley-LaPorte, John and Odette. *Chartres: Le Labyrinthe Déchiffré.* Éditions Jean-Michel Garnier, 1997.

Kidd, Sue Monk. "A Guiding Feminine Myth." In *The Dance of the Dissident Daughter.* San Francisco: HarperSanFrancisco, 1996.

Kraft, John. *The Goddess in the Labyrinth.* Gezeliusgatan, Finland: Abo Adademi, 1995.

"Labyrinth: The History of the Maze." Washington, D.C.: New River Media, 1996.

"Labyrinths: Their Mystery and Magic." Staatsburg, N.Y.: Penny Price Media, 1997.

Laishley, Barbara. "The Labyrinth as Ritual Action: An Examination of Efficacy, Intent, and Neurological Function." Unpublished paper, American Academy of Religion, San Francisco, November 1997.

Lanser, Taffy. "Grace Cathedral Labyrinth: A Rug beneath My Feet." *Labyrinth Letter* 1, no. 1 (April 1995): 11.

Lindsay, Tamar. "Labyrinth Structures: Four Walls, Back Doors, and Some Others." *Caerdroia* 28 (1997): 43–48.

———. "What's in a Name? Choices in the Unicursal Labyrinth: The Path versus the Wall." Parts 1 and 2. *Labyrinth Letter* 2, no. 2 (January 1996): 2–4; no. 3 (July 1996): 4–7.

Lonegren, Sig. "The Benton Castle Labyrinth." *Labyrinth Letter* 2, no. 4 (October 1996): 10–13.

———. "The Classical Seven Circuit Labyrinth: Coming to Terms." *Labyrinth Letter* 1, no. 1 (April 1995): 4–7.

———. "From Labyrinths to Mazes: The Stockholm Archipelago." *Caerdroia* 26 (1993): 39–43.

———. *Labyrinths: Ancient Myths and Modern Uses.* Glastonbury, Eng.: Gothic Image Publications, 1996.

Lundén, Staffan. "The Labyrinth in the Mediterranean: Part II." *Caerdroia* 28 (1997): 28–34.

———. "A Nepalese Labyrinth." *Caerdroia* 26 (1993): 13–19.

"Mazes and Labyrinths: Symbols of the Soul." In *The Atlas of Mysterious Places: The World's Unexplained Sacred Sites, Symbolic Landscapes, Ancient Cities, and Lost Lands,* edited by Jennifer Westwood. New York: Weidenfeld & Nicolson, 1987.

"Mazes and Labyrinths: The Search for the Center." Video. Cyclone Productions, 1996.

McMillen, Joan. "Remembering the Way: Ceremony in Honor of the Labyrinth at Chartres." Audiocassette. Menlo Park, Calif.: Joan Marie McMillen, 1989.

Oppenheimer, Max, Jr. "On Labyrinths and Mazes: Meanderings and Musings." *Labyrinth Letter* 1, no. 2 (July 1995): 4–6.

Pennick, Nigel. *Mazes and Labyrinths.* London: Robert Hale, 1990.

Rigoglioso, Marguerite. "The Oldest Labyrinth in the World? The Polyphemus Cave Paintings." *Caerdroia* 29 (1998): 14–22.

Saward, Jeff. *Ancient Labyrinths of the World.* Thundersley, Eng.: Caerdroia, 1997.

Taylor, Jeremy. *The Living Labyrinth: Exploring Universal Themes in Myth, Dreams, and the Symbolism of Daily Life.* Mahwah, N.J.: Paulist Press, 1998.

Villette, Jean. *The Enigma of the Labyrinth.* Trans. Robert Ferré and Ruth Hanna. St. Louis: One Way Press, 1995.

Weber, Susan. "What Is a Labyrinth?" *Labyrinth Letter* 2, no. 1 (January 1996): 24.